Metaphor —

speech in which a word
or phrase denoting one
kind of object or action
is used in place of another

Illness as Metaphor

to suggest likeness or
analogy between them.

— an implied
comparison in
contrast to explicit
comparison of
the simile

Illness
as Metaphor

SUSAN SONTAG

VINTAGE BOOKS
A Division of Random House
New York

FIRST VINTAGE BOOKS EDITION, June 1979

Library of Congress Cataloging in Publication Data
Sontag, Susan, 1933-
   Illness as metaphor.
   1. Tuberculosis in literature. 2. Tuberculosis
(in religion, folklore, etc.) 3. Cancer (in
religion, folklore, etc.) I. Title.
[PN56.T82S6 1979]   809′.933′5   78-23537
ISBN 0-394-72844-0

for Robert Silvers

Illness as Metaphor

Illness is the night-side of life, a more onerous citi-zenship. Everyone who is born holds dual citizenship, in the kingdom of the well and in the kingdom of the sick. Although we all prefer to use only the good pass-port, sooner or later each of us is obliged, at least for a spell, to identify ourselves as citizens of that other place.

I want to describe, not what it is really like to emi-grate to the kingdom of the ill and live there, but the punitive or sentimental fantasies concocted about that situation: not real geography, but stereotypes of na-tional character. My subject is not physical illness itself but the uses of illness as a figure or metaphor. My point is that illness is *not* a metaphor, and that the most truth-ful way of regarding illness—and the healthiest way of being ill—is one most purified of, most resistant to, metaphoric thinking. Yet it is hardly possible to take up one's residence in the kingdom of the ill unprejudiced by the lurid metaphors with which it has been land-scaped. It is toward an elucidation of those metaphors, and a liberation from them, that I dedicate this inquiry.

1

Two diseases have been spectacularly, and similarly, encumbered by the trappings of metaphor: tuberculosis and cancer.

The fantasies inspired by TB in the last century, by cancer now, are responses to a disease thought to be intractable and capricious—that is, a disease not understood—in an era in which medicine's central premise is that all diseases can be cured. Such a disease is, by definition, mysterious. For as long as its cause was not understood and the ministrations of doctors remained so ineffective, TB was thought to be an insidious, implacable theft of a life. Now it is cancer's turn to be the disease that doesn't knock before it enters, cancer fills the role of an illness experienced as a ruthless, secret invasion—a role it will keep until, one day, its etiology becomes as clear and its treatment as effective as those of TB have become.

Although the way in which disease mystifies is set against a backdrop of new expectations, the disease itself (once TB, cancer today) arouses thoroughly old-fashioned kinds of dread. Any disease that is treated as a mystery and acutely enough feared will be felt to be morally, if not literally, contagious. Thus, a surprisingly large number of people with cancer find themselves being shunned by relatives and friends and are the object of practices of decontamination by members of their household, as if cancer, like TB, were an infectious disease. Contact with someone afflicted with a disease regarded as a mysterious malevolency inevitably feels like a trespass; worse, like the violation of a taboo. The very names of such diseases are felt to have a magic power. In Stendhal's *Armance* (1827), the hero's mother refuses to say "tuberculosis," for fear that pronouncing the word will hasten the course of her son's malady. And Karl Menninger has observed (in *The Vital Balance*) that "the very word 'cancer' is said to kill some patients who would not have succumbed (so quickly) to the malignancy from which they suffer." This observation is offered in support of anti-intellectual pieties and a facile compassion all too triumphant in contemporary medicine and psychiatry. "Patients who consult us because of their suffering and their distress and their disability," he continues, "have every right to resent being plastered with a damning index tab." Dr. Menninger recommends that physicians generally abandon "names" and "labels" ("our function is to help these people, not to further afflict them")—which would mean, in effect, increasing secretiveness and medical paternalism. It is not naming as such that is pejorative or damning, but the name "cancer." As long as a particular disease is treated as an evil, invincible predator, not just a disease, most people with cancer will indeed be demoralized by learning what disease they have. The solution is hardly

6

to stop telling cancer patients the truth, but to rectify the conception of the disease, to de-mythicize it.

When, not so many decades ago, learning that one had TB was tantamount to hearing a sentence of death —as today, in the popular imagination, cancer equals death—it was common to conceal the identity of their disease from tuberculars and, after they died, from their children. Even with patients informed about their disease, doctors and family were reluctant to talk freely. "Verbally I don't learn anything definite," Kafka wrote to a friend in April 1924 from the sanatorium where he died two months later, "since in discussing tuberculosis . . . everybody drops into a shy, evasive, glassy-eyed manner of speech." Conventions of concealment with cancer are even more strenuous. In France and Italy it is still the rule for doctors to communicate a cancer diagnosis to the patient's family but not to the patient; doctors consider that the truth will be intolerable to all but exceptionally mature and intelligent patients. (A leading French oncologist has told me that fewer than a tenth of his patients know they have cancer.) In America—in part because of the doctors' fear of malpractice suits—there is now much more candor with patients, but the country's largest cancer hospital mails routine communications and bills to outpatients in envelopes that do not reveal the sender, on the assumption that the illness may be a secret from their families. Since getting cancer can be a scandal that jeopardizes one's love life, one's chance of promotion, even one's job, patients who know what they have tend to be extremely prudish, if not outright secretive, about their disease. And a federal law, the 1966 Freedom of Information Act, cites "treatment

7

for cancer" in a clause exempting from disclosure matters whose disclosure "would be an unwarranted invasion of personal privacy." It is the only disease mentioned.

All this lying to and by cancer patients is a measure of how much harder it has become in advanced industrial societies to come to terms with death. As death is now an offensively meaningless event, so that disease widely considered a synonym for death is experienced as something to hide. The policy of equivocating about the nature of their disease with cancer patients reflects the conviction that dying people are best spared the news that they are dying, and that the good death is the sudden one, best of all if it happens while we're unconscious or asleep. Yet the modern denial of death does not explain the extent of the lying and the wish to be lied to; it does not touch the deepest dread. Someone who has had a coronary is at least as likely to die of another one within a few years as someone with cancer is likely to die soon from cancer. But no one thinks of concealing the truth from a cardiac patient: there is nothing shameful about a heart attack. Cancer patients are lied to, not just because the disease is (or is thought to be) a death sentence, but because it is felt to be obscene—in the original meaning of that word: ill-omened, abominable, repugnant to the senses. Cardiac disease implies a weakness, trouble, failure that is mechanical; there is no disgrace, nothing of the taboo that once surrounded peoples afflicted with TB and still surrounds those who have cancer. The metaphors attached to TB and to cancer imply living processes of a particularly resonant and horrid kind.

8

2

Throughout most of their history, the metaphoric uses of TB and cancer crisscross and overlap. The *Oxford English Dictionary* records "consumption" in use as a synonym for pulmonary tuberculosis as early as 1398.* (John of Trevisa: "Whan the blode is made thynne, soo folowyth consumpcyon and wastyng.") But the pre-modern understanding of cancer also invokes the notion of consumption. The OED gives as the early figurative definition of cancer: "Anything that frets, corrodes, corrupts, or consumes slowly and secretly." (Thomas Paynell in 1528: "A canker is a melancolye impostume eatynge partes of the bodye.") The earliest literal definition of cancer is a growth, lump, or protuberance, and the disease's name—from the Greek *karkínos* and the Latin *cancer,* both meaning crab— was inspired, according to Galen, by the resemblance of

* Godefroy's *Dictionnaire de l'ancienne langue française* cites Bernard de Gordon's *Pratiqum* (1495): *"Tisis, c'est ung ulcere du polmon qui consume tout le corp."*

an external tumor's swollen veins to a crab's legs, not, as many people think, because a metastatic disease crawls or creeps like a crab. But etymology indicates that tuberculosis was also once considered a type of abnormal extrusion: the word tuberculosis—from the Latin *tūberculum,* the diminutive of *tūber,* bump, swelling—means a morbid swelling, protuberance, projection, or growth.* Rudolf Virchow, who founded the the science of cellular pathology in the 1850s, thought of the tubercle as a tumor.

Thus, from late antiquity until quite recently, tuberculosis was—typologically—cancer. And cancer was described, like TB, as a process in which the body was consumed. The modern conceptions of the two diseases could not be set until the advent of cellular pathology. Only with the microscope was it possible to grasp the distinctiveness of cancer, as a type of cellular activity, and to understand that the disease did not always take the form of an external or even palpable tumor. (Before the mid-nineteenth century, nobody could have identified leukemia as a form of cancer.) And it was not possible definitively to separate cancer from TB until after 1882, when tuberculosis was discovered to be a bacterial infection. Such advances in medical thinking enabled the leading metaphors of the

* The same etymology is given in the standard French dictionaries. *"La tubercule"* was introduced in the sixteenth century by Ambroise Paré from the Latin *tūberculum,* meaning *"petite bosse"* (little lump). In Diderot's *Encyclopédie,* the entry on tuberculosis (1765) cites the definition given by the English physician Richard Morton in his *Phthisiologia* (1689): *"des petits tumeurs qui paraissent sur la surface du corps."* In French, all tiny surface tumors were once called *"tubercules";* the word became limited to what we identify as TB only after Koch's discovery of the tubercle bacillus.

two diseases to become truly distinct and, for the most part, contrasting. The modern fantasy about the cancer could then begin to take shape—a fantasy which from the 1920s on would inherit most of the problems dramatized by the fantasies about TB, but with the two diseases and their symptoms conceived in quite different, almost opposing, ways.

•

1. TB is understood as a disease of one organ, the lungs, while cancer is understood as a disease that can turn up in any organ and whose outreach is the whole body.

2. TB is understood as a disease of extreme contrasts: white pallor and red flush, hyperactivity alternating with languidness. The spasmodic course of the disease is illustrated by what is thought of as the prototypical TB symptom, coughing. The sufferer is wracked by coughs, then sinks back, recovers breath, breathes normally; then coughs again. Cancer is a disease of growth (sometimes visible; more characteristically, inside), of abnormal, ultimately lethal growth that is measured, incessant, steady. Although there may be periods in which tumor growth is arrested (remissions), cancer produces no contrasts like the oxymorons of behavior—febrile activity, passionate resignation—thought to be typical of TB. The tubercular is pallid some of the time; the pallor of the cancer patient is unchanging.

3. TB makes the body transparent. The X-rays, which are the standard diagnostic tool, permit one, often for the first time, to see one's insides—to become trans-

11

parent to oneself. While TB is understood to be, from early on, rich in visible symptoms (progressive emaciation, coughing, languidness, fever), and can be suddenly and dramatically revealed (the blood on the handkerchief), in cancer the main symptoms are thought to be, characteristically, invisible—until the last stage, when it is too late. The disease, often discovered by chance or through a routine medical checkup, can be far advanced without exhibiting any appreciable symptoms. One has an opaque body that must be taken to a specialist to find out if it contains cancer. What the patient cannot perceive, the specialist will determine by analyzing tissues taken from the body. TB patients may see their X-rays or even possess them: the patients at the sanatorium in *The Magic Mountain* carry theirs around in their breast pockets. Cancer patients don't look at their biopsies.

TB was—still is—thought to produce spells of euphoria, increased appetite, exacerbated sexual desire. Part of the regimen for patients in *The Magic Mountain* is a second breakfast, eaten with gusto. Cancer is thought to cripple vitality, make eating an ordeal, deaden desire. Having TB was imagined to be an aphrodisiac, and to confer extraordinary powers of seduction. Cancer is considered to be de-sexualizing. But it is characteristic of TB that many of its symptoms are deceptive—liveliness that comes from enervation, rosy cheeks that look like a sign of health but come from fever—and an upsurge of vitality may be a sign of approaching death. (Such gushes of energy will generally be self-destructive, and may be destructive of others: recall the Old West legend of Doc Holliday, the tubercular gunfighter released from moral restraints by the

12

ravages of his disease.) Cancer has only true symptoms. TB is disintegration, febrilization, dematerialization; it is a disease of liquids—the body turning to phlegm and mucus and sputum and, finally, blood—and of air, of the need for better air. Cancer is degeneration, the body tissues turning to something hard. Alice James, writing in her journal a year before she died from cancer in 1892, speaks of "this unholy granite substance in my breast." But this lump is alive, a fetus with its own will. Novalis, in an entry written around 1798 for his encyclopedia project, defines cancers, along with gangrene, as "full-fledged *parasites*—they grow, are engendered, engender, have their structure, secrete, eat." Cancer is a demonic pregnancy. St. Jerome must have been thinking of a cancer when he wrote: "The one there with his swollen belly is pregnant with his own death" (*"Alius tumenti aqualiculo mortem parturit"*). Though the course of both diseases is emaciating, losing weight from TB is understood very differently from losing weight from cancer. In TB the person is "consumed," burned up. In cancer, the patient is "invaded" by alien cells, which multiply, causing an atrophy or blockage of bodily functions. The cancer patient "shrivels" (Alice James's word) or "shrinks" (Wilhelm Reich's word).

TB is a disease of time; it speeds up life, highlights it, spiritualizes it. In both English and French, consumption "gallops." Cancer has stages rather than gaits; it is (eventually) "terminal." Cancer works slowly, insidiously: the standard euphemism in obituaries is that someone has "died after a long illness." Every characterization of cancer describes it as slow, and so it was first used metaphorically. "The word of

13

hem crepith as a kankir," Wyclif wrote in 1382 (translating a phrase in II Timothy 2:17); and among the earliest figurative uses of cancer are as a metaphor for "idleness" and "sloth."* Metaphorically, cancer is not so much a disease of time as a disease or pathology of space. Its principal metaphors refer to topography (cancer "spreads" or "proliferates" or is "diffused"; tumors are surgically "excised"), and its most dreaded consequence, short of death, is the mutilation or amputation of part of the body.

TB is often imagined as a disease of poverty and deprivation—of thin garments, thin bodies, unheated rooms, poor hygiene, inadequate food. The poverty may not be as literal as Mimi's garret in *La Bohème*; the tubercular Marguerite Gautier in *La Dame aux camélias* lives in luxury, but inside she is a waif. In contrast, cancer is a disease of middle-class life, a disease associated with affluence, with excess. Rich countries have the highest cancer rates, and the rising incidence of the disease is seen as resulting, in part, from a diet rich in fat and proteins and from the toxic effluvia of the industrial economy that creates affluence. The treatment of TB is identified with the stimulation of appetite, cancer treatment with nausea and the loss of appetite. The undernourished nourishing themselves —alas, to no avail. The overnourished, unable to eat.

The TB patient was thought to be helped, even cured, by a change in environment. There was a notion that

* As cited in the OED, which gives as an early figurative use of "canker": "that pestilent and most infectious canker, idlenesse"—T. Palfreyman, 1564. And of "cancer" (which replaced "canker" around 1700): "Sloth is a Cancer, eating up that Time Princes should cultivate for Things sublime"—Edmund Ken, 1711.

14

TB was a wet disease, a disease of humid and dank cities. The inside of the body became damp ("moisture in the lungs" was a favored locution) and had to be dried out. Doctors advised travel to high, dry places— the mountains, the desert. But no change of surroundings is thought to help the cancer patient. The fight is all inside one's own body. It may be, is increasingly thought to be, something in the environment that has caused the cancer. But once cancer is present, it cannot be reversed or diminished by a move to a better (that is, less carcinogenic) environment.

TB is thought to be relatively painless. Cancer is thought to be, invariably, excruciatingly painful. TB is thought to provide an easy death, while cancer is the spectacularly wretched one. For over a hundred years TB remained the preferred way of giving death a meaning—an edifying, refined disease. Nineteenth-century literature is stocked with descriptions of almost symptomless, unfrightened, beatific deaths from TB, particularly of young people, such as Little Eva in *Uncle Tom's Cabin* and Dombey's son Paul in *Dombey and Son* and Smike in *Nicholas Nickleby,* where Dickens described TB as the "dread disease" which "refines" death.

> if its grosser aspect . . . in which the struggle between soul and body is so gradual, quiet, and solemn, and the result so sure, that day by day, and grain by grain, the mortal part wastes and withers away, so that the spirit grows light and sanguine with its lightening load. . . .*

* Nearly a century later, in his edition of Katherine Mansfield's posthumously published *Journal,* John Middleton Murry uses similar language to describe Mansfield on the last day of

15

Contrast these ennobling, placid TB deaths with the ignoble, agonizing cancer deaths of Eugene Gant's father in Thomas Wolfe's *Of Time and the River* and of the sister in Bergman's film *Cries and Whispers*. The dying tubercular is pictured as made more beautiful and more soulful; the person dying of cancer is portrayed as robbed of all capacities of self-transcendence, humiliated by fear and agony.

•

These are contrasts drawn from the popular mythology of both diseases. Of course, many tuberculars died in terrible pain, and some people die of cancer feeling little or no pain to the end; the poor and the rich both get TB and cancer; and not everyone who has TB coughs. But the mythology persists. It is not just because pulmonary tuberculosis is the most common form of TB that most people think of TB, in contrast to cancer, as a disease of one organ. It is because the myths about TB do not fit the brain, larynx, kidneys, long bones, and other sites where the tubercle bacillus can also settle, but do have a close fit with the traditional imagery (breath, life) associated with the lungs. While TB takes on qualities assigned to the lungs, which are part of the upper, spiritualized body, cancer is notorious for attacking parts of the body (colon,

---

her life. "I have never seen, nor shall I ever see, any one so beautiful as she was on that day; it was as though the exquisite perfection which was always hers had taken possession of her completely. To use her own words, the last grain of 'sediment,' the last 'traces of earthly degradation,' were departed for ever. But she had lost her life to save it."

bladder, rectum, breast, cervix, prostrate, testicles) that
are embarrassing to acknowledge. Having a tumor
generally arouses some feelings of shame, but in the
hierarchy of the body's organs, lung cancer is felt to be
less shameful than rectal cancer. And one non-tumor
form of cancer now turns up in commercial fiction in
the role once monopolized by TB, as the romantic
disease which cuts off a young life. (The heroine of
Erich Segal's *Love Story* dies of leukemia—the "white"
or TB-like form of the disease, for which no mutilating
surgery can be proposed—not of stomach or breast
cancer.) A disease of the lungs is, metaphorically, a
disease of the soul.* Cancer, as a disease that can
strike anywhere, is a disease of the body. Far from re-
vealing anything spiritual, it reveals that the body is,
all too woefully, just the body.

Such fantasies flourish because TB and cancer are
thought to be much more than diseases that usually are
(or were) fatal. They are identified with death itself.
In *Nicholas Nickleby*, Dickens apostrophized TB as the

disease in which death and life are so strangely
blended, that death takes the glow and hue of life, and

* The Goncourt brothers, in their novel *Madame Gervaisais*
(1869), called TB "this illness of the lofty and noble parts of
the human being," contrasting it with "the diseases of the crude,
base organs of the body, which clog and soil the patient's
mind. . . ." In Mann's early story "Tristan," the young wife has
tuberculosis of the trachea: ". . . the trachea, and not the lungs,
thank God! But it is a question whether, if it had been the lungs
the new patient could have looked any more pure and ethereal,
any remoter from the concerns of this world, than she did now
as she leaned back pale and weary in her chaste white-enamelled
arm-chair, beside her robust husband, and listened to the con-
versation."

17

life the gaunt and grisly form of death; disease which medicine never cured, wealth never warded off, or poverty could boast exemption from. . . .

And Kafka wrote to Max Brod in October 1917 that he had "come to think that tuberculosis . . . is no special disease, or not a disease that deserves a special name, but only the germ of death itself, intensified. . . ." Cancer inspires similar speculations. Georg Groddeck, whose remarkable views on cancer in *The Book of the It* (1923) anticipate those of Wilhelm Reich, wrote:

> Of all the theories put forward in connection with cancer, only one has in my opinion survived the passage of time, namely, that cancer leads through definite stages to death. I mean by that that what is not fatal is not cancer. From that you may conclude that I hold out no hope of a new method of curing cancer . . . [only] the many cases of so-called cancer. . . .

For all the progress in treating cancer, many people still subscribe to Groddeck's equation: cancer = death. But the metaphors surrounding TB and cancer reveal much about the idea of the morbid, and how it has evolved from the nineteenth century (when TB was the most common cause of death) to our time (when cancer is the most dreaded disease). The Romantics moralized death in a new way: with the TB death, which dissolved the gross body, etherealized the personality, expanded consciousness. It was equally possible, through fantasies about TB, to aestheticize death. Thoreau, who had TB, wrote in 1852: "Death and disease are often beautiful, like . . . the hectic glow of consumption." Nobody conceives of cancer the way

18

TB was thought of—as a decorative, often lyrical death. Cancer is a rare and still scandalous subject for poetry; and it seems unimaginable to aestheticize the disease.

3

The most striking similarity between the myths of TB and cancer is that both are, or were, understood as diseases of passion. Fever in TB was a sign of an inward burning: the tubercular is someone "consumed" by ardor, that ardor leading to the dissolution of the body. The use of metaphors drawn from TB to describe love—the image of a "diseased" love, of a passion that "consumes"—long antedates the Romantic movement.* Starting with the Romantics, the image was inverted, and TB was conceived as a variant of the disease of love. In a heartbreaking letter of November 1, 1820 from Naples, Keats, forever separated from Fanny Brawne, wrote, "If I had any chance of recovery [from tuberculosis], this passion would kill me." As a character in *The Magic Mountain* explains: "Symptoms of

---

* As in Act II, Scene 2 of Sir George Etherege's play *The Man of Mode* (1676): "When love grows diseas'd, the best thing we can do is to put it to a violent death; I cannot endure the torture of a lingring and consumptive passion."

disease are nothing but a disguised manifestation of the power of love; and all disease is only love transformed."

As once TB was thought to come from too much passion, afflicting the reckless and sensual, today many people believe that cancer is a disease of insufficient passion, afflicting those who are sexually repressed, inhibited, unspontaneous, incapable of expressing anger. These seemingly opposite diagnoses are actually not so different versions of the same view (and deserve, in my opinion, the same amount of credence). For both psychological accounts of a disease stress the insufficiency or the balking of vital energies. As much as TB was celebrated as a disease of passion, it was also regarded as a disease of repression. The high-minded hero of Gide's *The Immoralist* contracts TB (paralleling what Gide perceived to be his own story) because he has repressed his true sexual nature; when Michel accepts Life, he recovers. With this scenario, today, Michel would have to get cancer.

As cancer is now imagined to be the wages of repression, so TB was once explained as the ravages of frustration. What is called a liberated sexual life is believed by some people today to stave off cancer, for virtually the same reason that sex was often prescribed to tuberculars as a therapy. In *The Wings of the Dove,* Milly Theale's doctor advises a love affair as a cure for her TB; and it is when she discovers that her duplicitous suitor, Merton Densher, is secretly engaged to her friend Kate Croy that she dies. And in his letter of November 1820, Keats exclaimed: "My dear Brown, I should have had her when I was in health, and I should have remained well."

According to the mythology of TB, there is generally some passionate feeling which provokes, which expresses itself in, a bout of TB. But the passions must be thwarted, the hopes blighted. And the passion, although usually love, could be a political or moral passion. At the end of Turgenev's *On the Eve* (1860), Insarov, the young Bulgarian revolutionary-in-exile who is the hero of the novel, realizes that he can't return to Bulgaria. In a hotel in Venice, he sickens with longing and frustration, gets TB, and dies.

According to the mythology of cancer, it is generally a steady repression of feeling that causes the disease. In the earlier, more optimistic form of this fantasy, the repressed feelings were sexual; now in a notable shift, the repression of violent feelings is imagined to cause cancer. The thwarted passion that killed Insarov was idealism. The passion that people think will give them cancer if they don't discharge it is rage. There are no modern Insarovs. Instead, there are cancerphobes like Norman Mailer, who recently explained that had he not stabbed his wife (and acted out "a murderous nest of feeling") he would have gotten cancer and "been dead in a few years himself." It is the same fantasy that was once attached to TB, but in rather a nastier version.

The source for much of the current fancy that associates cancer with the repression of passion is Wilhelm Reich, who defined cancer as "a disease following emotional resignation—a bio-energetic shrinking, a giving up of hope." Reich illustrated his influential theory with Freud's cancer, which he thought began when Freud, naturally passionate and "very unhappily married," yielded to resignation:

He lived a very calm, quiet, decent family life, but there is little doubt that he was very much dissatisfied genitally. Both his resignation and his cancer were evidence of that. Freud had to give up, as a person. He had to give up his personal pleasures, his personal delights, in his middle years. . . . if my view of cancer is correct, you just give up, you resign—and, then, you shrink.

Tolstoy's "The Death of Ivan Ilyich" is often cited as a case history of the link between cancer and characterological resignation. But the same theory has been applied to TB by Groddeck, who defined TB as

the pining to die away. The desire must die away, then, the desire for the in and out, the up and down of erotic love, which is symbolized in breathing. And with the desire the lungs die away. . . . the body dies away. . . .*

As do accounts of cancer today, the typical accounts of TB in the nineteenth century all feature resignation as the cause of the disease. They also show how, as the disease advances, one *becomes* resigned—Mimi and Camille die because of their renunciation of love, beatified by resignation. Robert Louis Stevenson's autobiographical essay "Ordered South," written in 1874, describes the stages whereby the tubercular is "tenderly weaned from the passion of life," and an ostentatious resignation is characteristic of the rapid decline of tuberculars as reported at length in fiction. In *Uncle*

* The passage continues: ". . . because desire increases during the illness, because the guilt of the ever-repeated symbolic dissipation of semen in the sputum is continually growing greater, . . . because the It allows pulmonary disease to bring beauty to the eyes and cheek, alluring poisons!"

Tom's Cabin, Little Eva dies with preternatural serenity, announcing to her father a few weeks before the end: "My strength fades away every day, and I know I must go." All we learn of Milly Theale's death in *The Wings of the Dove* is that "she turned her face to the wall." TB was represented as the prototypical passive death. Often it was a kind of suicide. In Joyce's "The Dead," Michael Furey stands in the rain in Gretta Conroy's garden the night before she leaves for the convent school; she implores him to go home; "he said he did not want to live" and a week later he dies.

TB sufferers may be represented as passionate but are, more characteristically, deficient in vitality, in life force. (As in the contemporary updating of this fantasy, the cancer-prone are those who are not sufficiently sensual or in touch with their anger.) This is how those two famously tough-minded observers, the Goncourt brothers, explain the TB of their friend Murger (the author of *Scènes de la vie de Bohème*): he is dying "for want of vitality with which to withstand suffering." Michael Furey was "very delicate," as Gretta Conroy explains to her "stout, tallish," virile, suddenly jealous husband. TB is celebrated as the disease of born victims, of sensitive, passive people who are not quite life-loving enough to survive. (What is hinted at by the yearning but almost somnolent belles of Pre-Raphaelite art is made explicit in the emaciated, hollow-eyed, tubercular girls depicted by Edvard Munch.) And while the standard representation of a death from TB places the emphasis on the perfected sublimation of feeling, the recurrent figure of the tubercular courtesan indicates that TB was also thought to make the sufferer sexy.

Like all really successful metaphors, the metaphor of

TB was rich enough to provide for two contradictory applications. It described the death of someone (like a child) thought to be too "good" to be sexual: the assertion of an angelic psychology. It was also a way of describing sexual feelings—while lifting the responsibility for libertinism, which is blamed on a state of objective, physiological decadence or deliquescence. It was both a way of describing sensuality and promoting the claims of passion and a way of describing repression and advertising the claims of sublimation, the disease inducing both a "numbness of spirit" (Robert Louis Stevenson's words) and a suffusion of higher feelings. Above all, it was a way of affirming the value of being more conscious, more complex psychologically. Health becomes banal, even vulgar.

4

It seems that having TB had already acquired the associations of being romantic by the mid-eighteenth century. In Act I, Scene 1 of Oliver Goldsmith's satire on life in the provinces, *She Stoops to Conquer* (1773), Mr. Hardcastle is mildly remonstrating with Mrs. Hardcastle about how much she spoils her loutish son by a former marriage, Tony Lumpkin:

MRS. H.: And I am to blame? The poor boy was always too sickly to do any good. A school would be his death. When he comes to be a little stronger, who knows what a year or two's Latin may do for him?

MR. H.: Latin for him! A cat and fiddle. No, no, the ale-house and the stable are the only schools he'll ever go to.

MRS. H.: Well, we must not snub the poor boy now, for I believe we shan't have him long among us. Any body that looks in his face may see he's consumptive.

MR. H.: Ay, if growing too fat be one of the symptoms.

MRS. H.: He coughs sometimes.

MR. H.: Yes, when his liquor goes the wrong way.

MRS. H.: I'm actually afraid of his lungs.

MR. H.: And truly so am I; for he sometimes whoops like a speaking trumpet—[TONY *hallooing behind the Scenes*] —O there he goes—A very consumptive figure, truly.

This exchange suggests that the fantasy about TB was already a received idea, for Mrs. Hardcastle is nothing but an anthology of clichés of the smart London world to which she aspires, and which was the audience of Goldsmith's play.* Goldsmith presumes that the TB myth is already widely disseminated—TB being, as it were, the anti-gout. For snobs and parvenus and social climbers, TB was one index of being genteel, delicate, sensitive. With the new mobility (social and geographical) made possible in the eighteenth century, worth and station are not given; they must be asserted. They were asserted through new notions about clothes ("fashion") and new attitudes toward illness. Both clothes (the outer garment of the body) and illness (a kind of interior décor of the body) became tropes for new attitudes toward the self.

Shelley wrote on July 27, 1820 to Keats, commiserating as one TB sufferer to another, that he has learned "that you continue to wear a consumptive appearance." This was no mere turn of phrase. Consumption was understood as a manner of appearing, and that appearance became a staple of nineteenth-century man-

* Goldsmith, who was trained as a doctor and practiced medicine for a while, had other clichés about TB. In his essay "On Education" (1759) Goldsmith wrote that a diet lightly salted, sugared, and seasoned "corrects any consumptive habits, not unfrequently found amongst the children of city parents." Consumption is viewed as a habit, a disposition (if not an affectation), a weakness that must be strengthened and to which city people are more disposed.

ners. It became rude to eat heartily. It was glamorous to look sickly. "Chopin was tubercular at a time when good health was not chic," Camille Saint-Saëns wrote in 1913. "It was fashionable to be pale and drained; Princess Belgiojoso strolled along the boulevards . . . pale as death in person." Saint-Saëns was right to connect an artist, Chopin, with the most celebrated *femme fatale* of the period, who did a great deal to popularize the tubercular look. The TB-influenced idea of the body was a new model for aristocratic looks—at a moment when aristocracy stops being a matter of power, and starts being mainly a matter of image. ("One can never be too rich. One can never be too thin," the Duchess of Windsor once said.) Indeed, the romanticizing of TB is the first widespread example of that distinctively modern activity, promoting the self as an image. The tubercular look had to be considered attractive once it came to be considered a mark of distinction, of breeding. "I cough continually!" Marie Bashkirtsev wrote in the once widely read *Journal*, which was published, after her death at twenty-four, in 1887. "But for a wonder, far from making me look ugly, this gives me an air of languor that is very becoming." What was once the fashion of aristocratic *femmes fatales* and aspiring young artists became, eventually, the province of fashion as such. Twentieth-century women's fashions (with their cult of thinness) are the last stronghold of the metaphors associated with the romanticizing of TB in the late eighteenth and early nineteenth centuries.

Many of the literary and erotic attitudes known as "romantic agony" derive from tuberculosis and its

28

transformations through metaphor. Agony became romantic in a stylized account of the disease's preliminary symptoms (for example, debility is transformed into languor) and the actual agony was simply suppressed. Wan, hollow-chested young women and pallid, rachitic young men vied with each other as candidates for this mostly (at that time) incurable, disabling, really awful disease. "When I was young," wrote Théophile Gautier, "I could not have accepted as a lyrical poet anyone weighing more than ninety-nine pounds." (Note that Gautier says lyrical poet, apparently resigned to the fact that novelists had to be made of coarser and bulkier stuff.) Gradually, the tubercular look, which symbolized an appealing vulnerability, a superior sensitivity, became more and more the ideal look for women— while great men of the mid- and late nineteenth century grew fat, founded industrial empires, wrote hundreds of novels, made wars, and plundered continents.

One might reasonably suppose that this romanticization of TB was a merely literary transfiguration of the disease, and that in the era of its great depredations TB was probably thought to be disgusting—as cancer is now. Surely everyone in the nineteenth century knew about, for example, the stench in the breath of the consumptive person. (Describing their visit to the dying Murger, the Goncourts note "the odor of rotting flesh in his bedroom.") Yet all the evidence indicates that the cult of TB was not simply an invention of romantic poets and opera librettists but a widespread attitude, and that the person dying (young) of TB really was perceived as a romantic personality. One must suppose that the reality of this terrible disease

29

was no match for important new ideas, particularly about individuality. It is with TB that the idea of individual illness was articulated, along with the idea that people are made more conscious as they confront their deaths, and in the images that collected around the disease one can see emerging a modern idea of individuality that has taken in the twentieth century a more aggressive, if no less narcissistic, form. Sickness was a way of making people "interesting"—which is how "romantic" was originally defined. (Schlegel, in his essay "On the Study of Greek Poetry" [1795], offers "the interesting" as the ideal of modern—that is, romantic—poetry.) "The ideal of perfect health," Novalis wrote in a fragment from the period 1799–1800, "is only scientifically interesting"; what is really interesting is sickness, "which belongs to individualizing." This idea—of how interesting the sick are—was given its boldest and most ambivalent formulation by Nietzsche in *The Will to Power* and other writings, and though Nietzsche rarely mentioned a specific illness, those famous judgments about individual weakness and cultural exhaustion or decadence incorporate and extend many of the clichés about TB.

The romantic treatment of death asserts that people were made singular, made more interesting, by their illnesses. "I look pale," said Byron, looking into the mirror. "I should like to die of a consumption." "Why?" asked a friend, who was visiting Byron in Athens in October 1810. "Because the ladies would all say, 'Look at that poor Byron, how interesting he looks in dying.'" Perhaps the main gift to sensibility made by the Romantics is not thé aesthetics of cruelty and the beauty of the morbid (as Mario Praz suggested in his famous book),

30

or even the demand for unlimited personal liberty, but the nihilistic and sentimental idea of "the interesting."

•

Sadness made one "interesting." It was a mark of refinement, of sensibility, to be sad. That is, to be powerless. In Stendhal's *Armance,* the anxious mother is reassured by the doctor that Octave is not, after all, suffering from tuberculosis but only from that "dissatisfied and critical melancholy characteristic of young people of his generation and position." Sadness and tuberculosis became synonymous. The Swiss writer Henri Amiel, himself tubercular, wrote in 1852 in his *Journal intime*:

> Sky draped in gray, pleated by subtle shading, mists trailing on the distant mountains; nature despairing, leaves falling on all sides like the lost illusions of youth under the tears of incurable grief. . . . The fir tree, alone in its vigor, green, stoical in the midst of this universal tuberculosis.

But it takes a sensitive person to feel such sadness; or by implication, to contract tuberculosis. The myth of TB constitutes the next-to-last episode in the long career of the ancient idea of melancholy—which was the artist's disease, according to the theory of the four humours. The melancholy character—or the tubercular —was a superior one: sensitive, creative, a being apart. Keats and Shelley may have suffered atrociously from the disease. But Shelley consoled Keats that "this consumption is a disease particularly fond of people who write such good verses as you have done. . . ." So well

31

established was the cliché which connected TB and creativity that at the end of the century one critic suggested that it was the progressive disappearance of TB which accounted for the current decline of literature and the arts.

But the myth of TB provided more than an account of creativity. It supplied an important model of bohemian life, lived with or without the vocation of the artist. The TB sufferer was a dropout, a wanderer in endless search of the healthy place. Starting in the early nineteenth century, TB became a new reason for exile, for a life that was mainly traveling. (Neither travel nor isolation in a sanatorium was a form of treatment for TB before then.) There were special places thought to be good for tuberculars: in the early nineteenth century, Italy; then, islands in the Mediterranean or the South Pacific; in the twentieth century, the mountains, the desert—all landscapes that had themselves been successively romanticized. Keats was advised by his doctors to move to Rome; Chopin tried the islands of the western Mediterranean; Robert Louis Stevenson chose a Pacific exile; D. H. Lawrence roamed over half the globe.* The Romantics invented invalidism as a pretext

* "By a curious irony," Stevenson wrote, "the places to which we are sent when health deserts us are often singularly beautiful . . . [and] I daresay the sick man is not very inconsolable when he receives sentence of banishment, and is inclined to regard his ill-health as not the least fortunate accident of his life." But the experience of such enforced banishment, as Stevenson went on to describe it, was something less agreeable. The tubercular cannot enjoy his good fortune: "the world is disenchanted for him."

Katherine Mansfield wrote: "I seem to spend half of my life arriving at strange hotels. . . . The strange door shuts upon the stranger, and then I slip down in the sheets. Waiting for the for leisure, and for dismissing bourgeois obligations in order to live only for one's art. It was a way of retiring from the world without having to take responsibility for the decision—the story of *The Magic Mountain.* After passing his exams and before taking up his job in a Hamburg ship-building firm, young Hans Castorp makes a three-week visit to his tubercular cousin in the sanatorium at Davos. Just before Hans "goes down," the doctor diagnoses a spot on his lungs. He stays on the mountain for the next seven years.

By validating so many possibly subversive longings and turning them into cultural pieties, the TB myth survived irrefutable human experience and accumulating medical knowledge for nearly two hundred years. Although there was a certain reaction against the Romantic cult of the disease in the second half of the last century, TB retained most of its romantic attributes—as the sign of a superior nature, as a becoming frailty—through the end of the century and well into ours. It is still the sensitive young artist's disease in O'Neill's *Long Day's Journey into Night.* Kafka's letters are a compendium of speculations about the meaning of tuberculosis, as is *The Magic Mountain,* published in 1924, the year Kafka died. Much of the irony of *The Magic Mountain* turns on Hans Castorp, the stolid burgher, getting TB, the artist's disease—for Mann's

shadows to come out of the corners and spin their slow, slow web over the Ugliest Wallpaper of All. . . . The man in the room next to mine has the same complaint as I. When I wake in the night I hear him turning. And then he coughs. And after a silence I cough. And he coughs again. This goes on for a long time. Until I feel we are like two roosters calling each other at false dawns. From far-away hidden farms."

novel is a late, self-conscious commentary on the myth of TB. But the novel still reflects the myth: the burgher *is* indeed spiritually refined by his disease. To die of TB was still mysterious and (often) edifying and remained so until practically nobody in Western Europe and North America died of it any more. Although the incidence of the disease began to decline precipitously after 1900 because of improved hygiene, the mortality rate among those who contracted it remained high; the power of the myth was dispelled only when proper treatment was finally developed, with the discovery of streptomycin in 1944 and the introduction of isoniazid in 1952.

If it is still difficult to imagine how the reality of such a dreadful disease could be transformed so preposterously, it may help to consider our own era's comparable act of distortion, under the pressure of the need to express romantic attitudes about the self. The object of distortion is not, of course, cancer—a disease which nobody has managed to glamorize (though it fulfills some of the functions as a metaphor that TB did in the nineteenth century). In the twentieth century, the repellent, harrowing disease that is made the index of a superior sensitivity, the vehicle of "spiritual" feelings and "critical" discontent, is insanity.

The fancies associated with tuberculosis and insanity have many parallels. With both illnesses, there is confinement. Sufferers are sent to a "sanatorium" (the common word for a clinic for tuberculars and the most common euphemism for an insane asylum). Once put away, the patient enters a duplicate world with special rules. Like TB, insanity is a kind of exile. The metaphor of the psychic voyage is an extension of the romantic

34

idea of travel that was associated with tuberculosis. To be cured, the patient has to be taken out of his or her daily routine. It is not an accident that the most common metaphor for an extreme psychological experience viewed positively—whether produced by drugs or by becoming psychotic—is a trip.

In the twentieth century the cluster of metaphors and attitudes formerly attached to TB split up and are parceled out to two diseases. Some features of TB go to insanity: the notion of the sufferer as a hectic, reckless creature of passionate extremes, someone too sensitive to bear the horrors of the vulgar, everyday world. Other features of TB go to cancer—the agonies that can't be romanticized. Not TB but insanity is the current vehicle of our secular myth of self-transcendence. The romantic view is that illness exacerbates consciousness. Once that illness was TB; now it is insanity that is thought to bring consciousness to a state of paroxysmic enlightenment. The romanticizing of madness reflects in the most vehement way the contemporary prestige of irrational or rude (spontaneous) behavior (acting-out), of that very passionateness whose repression was once imagined to cause TB, and is now thought to cause cancer.

5

In "Death in Venice," passion brings about the collapse of all that has made Gustav von Aschenbach singular—his reason, his inhibitions, his fastidiousness. And disease further reduces him. At the end of the story, Aschenbach is just another cholera victim, his last degradation being to succumb to the disease afflicting so many in Venice at that moment. When in *The Magic Mountain* Hans Castorp is discovered to have tuberculosis, it is a promotion. His illness will make Hans become more singular, will make him more intelligent than he was before. In one fiction, disease (cholera) is the penalty for a secret love; in the other disease (TB) is its expression. Cholera is the kind of fatality that, in retrospect, has simplified a complex self, reducing it to sick environment. The disease that individualizes, that sets a person in relief against the environment, is tuberculosis.

What once made TB seem so "interesting"—or, as it was usually put, romantic—also made it a curse and a source of special dread. In contrast to the great epidemic diseases of the past (bubonic plague, typhus, cholera), which strike each person as a member of an afflicted community, TB was understood as a disease that isolates one from the community. However steep its incidence in a population, TB—like cancer today—always seemed to be a mysterious disease of individuals, a deadly arrow that could strike anyone, that singled out its victims one by one.

As after a cholera death, it used to be common practice to burn the clothes and other effects of someone who died of TB. "Those brutal Italians have nearly finished their monstrous business," Keats's companion Joseph Severn wrote from Rome on March 6, 1821, two weeks after Keats died in the little room on the Piazza di Spagna. "They have burned all the furniture—and are now scraping the walls—making new windows—new doors—and even a new floor." But TB was frightening, not only as a contagion, like cholera, but as a seemingly arbitrary, uncommunicable "taint." And people could believe that TB was inherited (think of the disease's recurrence in the families of Keats, the Brontës, Emerson, Thoreau, Trollope) and also believe that it revealed something singular about the person afflicted. In a similar way, the evidence that there are cancer-prone families and, possibly, a hereditary factor in cancer can be acknowledged without disturbing the belief that cancer is a disease that strikes each person, punitively, as an individual. No one asks "Why me?" who gets cholera or typhus. But "Why me?" (meaning "it's not fair") is the question of many who learn they have cancer.

However much TB was blamed on poverty and insalubrious surroundings, it was still thought that a certain inner disposition was needed in order to contract the disease. Doctors and laity believed in a TB character type—as now the belief in a cancer-prone character type, far from being confined to the back yard of folk superstition, passes for the most advanced medical thinking. In contrast to the modern bogey of the cancer-prone character—someone unemotional, inhibited, repressed—the TB-prone character that haunted imaginations in the nineteenth century was an amalgam of two different fantasies: someone both passionate and repressed.

That other notorious scourge among nineteenth-century diseases, syphilis, was at least not mysterious. Contracting syphilis was a predictable consequence, the consequence, usually, of having sex with a carrier of the disease. So, among all the guilt-embroidered fantasies about sexual pollution attached to syphilis, there was no place for a type of personality supposed to be especially susceptible to the disease (as was once imagined for TB and is now for cancer). The syphilitic personality type was someone who had the disease (Osvald in Ibsen's *Ghosts*, Adrian Leverkühn in *Doctor Faustus*), not someone who was likely to get it. In its role as scourge, syphilis implied a moral judgment (about off-limits sex, about prostitution) but not a psychological one. TB, once so mysterious—as cancer is now—suggested judgments of a deeper kind, both moral and psychological, about the ill.

•

The speculations of the ancient world made disease most often an instrument of divine wrath. Judgment was meted out either to a community (the plague in Book I of the *Iliad* that Apollo inflicts on the Achaeans in punishment for Agamemnon's abduction of Chryses' daughter; the plague in Oedipus that strikes Thebes because of the polluting presence of the royal sinner) or to a single person (the stinking wound in Philoctetes' foot). The diseases around which the modern fantasies have gathered—TB, cancer—are viewed as forms of self-judgment, of self-betrayal.

One's mind betrays one's body. "My head and lungs have come to an agreement without my knowledge," Kafka said about his TB in a letter to Max Brod in September 1917. Or one's body betrays one's feelings, as in Mann's late novel *The Black Swan,* whose aging heroine, youthfully in love with a young man, takes as the return of her menses what is actually a hemorrhage and the symptom of incurable cancer. The body's treachery is thought to have its own inner logic. Freud was "very beautiful . . . when he spoke," Wilhelm Reich reminisced. "Then it hit him just here, in the mouth. And that is where my interest in cancer began." That interest led Reich to propose his version of the link between a mortal disease and the character of those it humiliates.

In the pre-modern view of disease, the role of character was confined to one's behavior after its onset. Like any extreme situation, dreaded illnesses bring out both people's worst and best. The standard accounts of epidemics, however, are mainly of the devastating effect of disease upon character. The weaker the chronicler's preconception of disease as a punishment for wickedness, the more likely that the account will stress the moral corruption made manifest by the disease's spread.

Even if the disease is not thought to be a judgment on the community, it becomes one—retroactively—as it sets in motion an inexorable collapse of morals and manners. Thucydides relates the ways in which the plague that broke out in Athens in 430 B.C. spawned disorder and lawlessness ("The pleasure of the moment took the place both of honor and expedience") and corrupted language itself. And the whole point of Boccaccio's description in the first pages of the *Decameron* of the great plague of 1348 is how badly the citizens of Florence behaved.

In contrast to this disdainful knowledge of how most loyalties and loves shatter in the panic produced by epidemic disease, the accounts of modern diseases —where the judgment tends to fall on the individual rather than the society—seem exaggeratedly unaware of how poorly many people take the news that they are dying. Fatal illness has always been viewed as a test of moral character, but in the nineteenth century there is a great reluctance to let anybody flunk the test. And the virtuous only become more so as they slide toward death. This is standard achievement for TB deaths in fiction, and goes with the inveterate spiritualizing of TB and the sentimentalizing of its horrors. Tuberculosis provided a redemptive death for the fallen, like the young prostitute Fantine in *Les Misérables,* or a sacrificial death for the virtuous, like the heroine of Selma Lagerlöf's *The Phantom Chariot*. Even the ultra-virtuous, when dying of this disease, boost themselves to new moral heights. *Uncle Tom's Cabin*: Little Eva during her last days urges her father to become a serious Christian and free his slaves. *The Wings of the Dove*: after learning that her suitor is a fortune hunter,

Milly Theale wills her fortune to him and dies. *Dombey and Son*: "From some hidden reason, very imperfectly understood by himself—if understood at all—[Paul] felt a gradually increasing impulse of affection, towards almost everything and everybody in the place."

For those characters treated less sentimentally, the disease is viewed as the occasion finally to behave well. At the least, the calamity of disease can clear the way for insight into lifelong self-deceptions and failures of character. The lies that muffle Ivan Ilyich's drawn-out agony—his cancer being unmentionable to his wife and children—reveal to him the lie of his whole life; when dying, he is, for the first time, in a state of truth. The sixty-year-old civil servant in Kurosawa's film *Ikiru* (1952) quits his job after learning he has terminal stomach cancer and, taking up the cause of a slum neighborhood, fights the bureaucracy he had served. With one year left to live, Watanabe wants to do something that is worthwhile, wants to redeem his mediocre life.

6

Disease occurs in the *Iliad* and the *Odyssey* as supernatural punishment, as demonic possession, and as the result of natural causes. For the Greeks, disease could be gratuitous or it could be deserved (for a personal fault, a collective transgression, or a crime of one's ancestors). With the advent of Christianity, which imposed more moralized notions of disease, as of everything else, a closer fit between disease and "victim" gradually evolved. The idea of disease as punishment yielded the idea that a disease could be a particularly appropriate and just punishment. Cresseid's leprosy in Henryson's *The Testament of Cresseid* and Madame de Merteuil's smallpox in *Les Liaisons dangereuses* show the true face of the beautiful liar—a most involuntary revelation.

In the nineteenth century, the notion that the disease fits the patient's character, as the punishment fits the sinner, was replaced my the notion that it expresses character. Disease can be challenged by the will. "The

42

will exhibits itself as organized body," wrote Schopenhauer, but he denied that the will itself could be sick. Recovery from a disease depends on the will assuming "dictatorial power in order to subsume the rebellious forces" of the body. One generation earlier, a great physician, Bichat, had used a similar image, calling health "the silence of organs," disease "their revolt." Disease is what speaks through the body, a language for dramatizing the mental: a form of self-expression. Groddeck described illness as "a symbol, a representation of something going on within, a drama staged by the It. . . ."*

According to the pre-modern ideal of a well-balanced character, expressiveness is supposed to be limited. Behavior is defined by its potentiality for excess. Thus, when Kant makes figurative use of cancer, it is a metaphor for excess feeling. "Passions are cancers for pure practical reason and often incurable," Kant wrote in *Anthropologie* (1798). "The passions are . . . unfortunate moods that are pregnant with many evils," he added, evoking the ancient metaphoric connection between cancer and a pregnancy. When Kant compares passions (that is, extreme feelings) to cancers, he is of course using the pre-modern sense of the disease and a pre-Romantic evaluation of passion. Soon, turbulent feeling was to be viewed much more positively. "There

* Kafka, after his TB was diagnosed in September 1917, wrote in his diary: ". . . the infection in your lungs is only a symbol," the symbol of an emotional "wound whose inflammation is called F[elice]. . . ." To Max Brod he wrote: "the illness is speaking for me because I have asked it to do so"; and to Felice: "Secretly I don't believe this illness to be tuberculosis, at least not primarily tuberculosis, but rather a sign of my general bankruptcy."

43

is no one in the world less able to conceal his feelings than Emile," said Rousseau—meaning it as a compliment.

As excess feelings become positive, they are no longer analogized—in order to denigrate them—to a terrible disease. Instead, disease is seen as the vehicle of excess feeling. TB is the disease that makes manifest intense desire; that discloses, in spite of the reluctance of the individual, what the individual does not want to reveal. The contrast is no longer between moderate passions and excessive ones but between hidden passions and those which are brought into the open. Illness reveals desires of which the patient probably was unaware. Diseases—and patients—become subjects for decipherment. And these hidden passions are now considered a source of illness. "He who desires but acts not, breeds pestilence," Blake wrote: one of his defiant Proverbs of Hell.

The early Romantic sought superiority by desiring, and by desiring to desire, more intensely than others do. The inability to realize these ideals of vitality and perfect spontaneity was thought to make someone an ideal candidate for TB. Contemporary romanticism starts from the inverse principle—that it is others who desire intensely, and that it is oneself (the narratives are typically in the first person) who has little or no desire at all. There are precursors of the modern romanitc egos of unfeeling in nineteenth-century Russian novels (Pechorin in Lermontov's *A Hero of Our Time*, Stavrogin in *The Possessed*); but they are still heroes— restless, bitter, self-destructive, tormented by their inability to feel. (Even their glum, merely self-absorbed descendants, Roquentin in Sartre's *Nausea* and Meursault in Camus's *The Stranger*, seemed bewildered by their inability to feel.) The passive, affectless anti-hero who dominates contemporary American fiction is a creature of regular routines or unfeeling debauch; not self-destructive but prudent; not moody, dashing, cruel, just dissociated. The ideal candidate, according to contemporary mythology, for cancer.

•

Ceasing to consider disease as a punishment which fits the objective moral character, making it an expression of the inner self, might seem less moralistic. But this view turns out to be just as, or even more, moralistic and punitive. With the modern diseases (once TB, now cancer), the romantic idea that the disease expresses the character is invariably extended to assert that the character causes the disease—because it has not expressed itself. Passion moves inward, striking and blighting the deepest cellular recesses.

"The sick man himself creates his disease," Groddeck wrote; "he is the cause of the disease and we need seek none other." "Bacilli" heads Groddeck's list of mere "external causes"—followed by "chills, overeating, overdrinking, work, and anything else." He insists that it is "because it is not pleasant to look within ourselves" that doctors prefer to "attack the outer causes with prophylaxis, disinfection, and so on," rather than address the real, internal causes. In Karl Menninger's more recent formulation: "Illness is in part what the world has done to a victim, but in larger part it is what the victim has done with his world, and with himself. . . ." Such preposterous and dangerous views

manage to put the onus of the disease on the patient
and not only weaken the patient's ability to understand the range of plausible medical treatment but
also, implicitly, direct the patient away from such treatment. Cure is thought to depend principally on the
patient's already sorely tested or enfeebled capacity for
self-love. A year before her death in 1923, Katherine
Mansfield wrote in her *Journal*:

> A bad day. . . . horrible pains and so on, and weakness.
> I could do nothing. The weakness was not only physi-
> cal. I *must heal my Self* before I will be well. . . . This
> must be done alone and at once. It is at the root of my
> not getting better. My mind is not *controlled*.

Mansfield not only thinks it was the "Self" which made
her sick but thinks that she has a chance of being cured
of her hopelessly advanced lung disease if she could
heal that "Self."*

Both the myth about TB and the current myth about
cancer propose that one is responsible for one's disease.
But the cancer imagery is far more punishing. Given
the romantic values in use for judging character and
disease, some glamour attaches to having a disease
thought to come from being full of passion. But there
is mostly shame attached to a disease thought to stem
from the repression of emotion—an opprobrium echoed

---

* Mansfield, wrote John Middleton Murry, "had come to the
conviction that her bodily health depended upon her spiritual
condition. Her mind was henceforth preoccupied with discover-
ing some way to 'cure her soul'; and she eventually resolved,
to my regret, to abandon her treatment and to live as though
her grave physical illness were incidental, and even, so far as
she could, as though it were nonexistent."

46

in the views propagated by Groddeck and Reich, and the many writers influenced by them. The view of cancer as a disease of the failure of expressiveness condemns the cancer patient: expresses pity but also conveys contempt. Miss Gee, in Auden's poem from the 1930s, "passed by the loving couples" and "turned her head away." Then:

> Miss Gee knelt down in the side-aisle,
>   She knelt down on her knees;
> 'Lead me not into temptation
>   But make me a good girl, please.'
>
> The days and nights went by her
>   Like waves round a Cornish wreck;
> She bicycled down to the doctor
>   With her clothes buttoned up to her neck.
>
> She bicycled down to the doctor,
>   And rang the surgery bell;
> 'O, doctor, I've pain inside me,
>   And I don't feel very well.'
>
> Doctor Thomas looked her over,
>   And then he looked some more;
> Walked over to his wash-basin,
>   Said, 'Why didn't you come before?'
>
> Doctor Thomas sat over his dinner,
>   Though his wife was waiting to ring,
> Rolling his bread into pellets;
>   Said, 'Cancer's a funny thing.
>
> 'Nobody knows what the cause is,
>   Though some pretend they do;
> It's like some hidden assassin
>   Waiting to strike at you.

'Childless women get it,
    And men when they retire;
It's as if there had to be some outlet
    For their foiled creative fire.' . . .

The tubercular could be an outlaw or a misfit; the cancer personality is regarded more simply, and with condescension, as one of life's losers. Napoleon, Ulysses S. Grant, Robert A. Taft, and Hubert Humphrey have all had their cancer diagnosed as the reaction to political defeat and the curtailing of their ambitions. And the cancer deaths of those harder to describe as losers, like Freud and Wittgenstein, have been diagnosed as the gruesome penalty exacted for a lifetime of instinctual renunciation. (Few remember that Rimbaud died of cancer.) In contrast, the disease that claimed the likes of Keats, Poe, Chekhov, Simone Weil, Emily Brontë, and Jean Vigo was as much apotheosis as a verdict of failure.

7

Cancer is generally thought an inappropriate disease for a romantic character, in contrast to tuberculosis, perhaps because unromantic depression has supplanted the romantic notion of melancholy. "A fitful strain of melancholy," Poe wrote, "will ever be found inseparable from the perfection of the beautiful." Depression is melancholy minus its charms—the animation, the fits.

Supporting the theory about the emotional causes of cancer, there is a growing literature and body of research: and scarcely a week passes without a new article announcing to some general public or other the scientific link between cancer and painful feelings. Investigations are cited—most articles refer to the same ones—in which out of, say, several hundred cancer patients, two-thirds or three-fifths report being depressed or unsatisfied with their lives, and having suffered from the loss (through death or rejection or separation) of a parent, lover, spouse, or close friend. But it seems likely that of several hundred people who do *not* have cancer, most would also report depressing emotions and past traumas: this is called the human condition. And these case histories are recounted in a particularly forthcoming language of despair, of discontent about and obsessive preoccupation with the isolated self and its never altogether satisfactory "relationships," which bears the unmistakable stamp of our consumer culture. It is a language many Americans now use about themselves.*

Investigations carried out by a few doctors in the last century showed a high correlation between cancer and that era's complaints. In contrast to contemporary

* A study by Dr. Caroline Bedell Thomas of the Johns Hopkins University School of Medicine was thus summarized in one recent newspaper article ("Can Your Personality Kill You?"): "In brief, cancer victims are low-gear persons, seldom prey to outbursts of emotion. They have feelings of isolation from their parents dating back to childhood." Drs. Claus and Marjorie Bahnson at the Eastern Pennsylvania Psychiatric Institute have "charted a personality pattern of denial of hostility, depression and of memory of emotional deprivation in childhood" and "difficulty in maintaining close relationships." Dr. O. Carl Simonton, a radiologist in Fort Worth, Texas, who gives patients both radiation and psychotherapy, describes the cancer personality as someone with "a great tendency for self-pity and a markedly impaired ability to make and maintain meaningful relationships." Lawrence LeShan, a New York psychologist and psychotherapist (*You Can Fight for Your Life: Emotional Factors in the Causation of Cancer* [1977]), claims that "there is a general type of personality configuration among the majority of cancer patients" and a world-view that cancer patients share and "which pre-dates the development of cancer." He divides "the basic emotional pattern of the cancer patient" into three parts: "a childhood or adolescence marked by feelings of isolation," the loss of the "meaningful relationship" found in adulthood, and a subsequent "conviction that life holds no more hope." "The cancer patient," LeShan writes, "almost invariably is contemptuous of himself, and of his abilities and possibilities." Cancer patients are "empty of feeling and devoid of self."

American cancer patients, who invariably report having feelings of isolation and loneliness since childhood, Victorian cancer patients described overcrowded lives, burdened with work and family obligations, and bereavements. These patients don't express discontent with their lives as such or speculate about the quality of its satisfactions and the possibility of a "meaningful relationship." Physicians found the causes or predisposing factors of their patients' cancers in grief, in worry (noted as most acute among businessmen and the mothers of large families), in straitened economic circumstances and sudden reversals of fortune, and in overwork—or, if the patients were successful writers or politicians, in grief, rage, intellectual overexertion, the anxiety that accompanies ambition, and the stress of public life.*

Nineteenth-century cancer patients were thought to get the disease as the result of hyperactivity and hyperintensity. They seemed to be full of emotions that had

* "Always much trouble and hard work" is a notation that occurs in many of the brief case histories in Herbert Snow's *Clinical Notes on Cancer* (1883). Snow was a surgeon in the Cancer Hospital in London, and most of the patients he saw were poor. A typical observation: "Of 140 cases of breast-cancer, 103 gave an account of previous mental trouble, hard work, or other debilitating agency. Of 187 uterine ditto, 91 showed a similar history." Doctors who saw patients who led more comfortable lives made other observations. The physician who treated Alexandre Dumas for cancer, G. von Schmitt, published a book on cancer in 1871 in which he listed "deep and sedentary study and pursuits, and feverish and anxious agitation of public life, the cares of ambition, frequent paroxysms of rage, violent grief" as "the principal causes" of the disease. Quoted in Samuel J. Kowal, M.D., "Emotions as a Cause of Cancer: 18th and 19th Century Contributions," *Review of Psychoanalysis*, 42, 3 (July 1955).

to be damped down. As a prophylaxis against cancer, one English doctor urged his patients "to avoid over-taxing their strength, and to bear the ills of life with equanimity; above all things, not to 'give way' to any grief." Such stoic counsels have now been replaced by prescriptions for self-expression, from talking it out to the primal scream. In 1885, a Boston doctor advised "those who have apparently benign tumors in the breast of the advantage of being cheerful." Today, this would be regarded as encouraging the sort of emotional disso-ciation now thought to predispose people to cancer.

Popular accounts of the psychological aspects of cancer often cite old authorities, starting with Galen, who observed that "melancholy women" are more likely to get breast cancer than "sanguine women." But the meanings have changed. Galen (second century A.D.) meant by melancholy a physiological condition with complex characterological symptoms; we mean a mere mood. "Grief and anxiety," said the English surgeon Sir Astley Cooper in 1845, are among "the most fre-quent causes" of breast cancer. But the nineteenth-century observations undermine rather than support late-twentieth-century notions—evoking a manic or manic-depressive character type almost the opposite of that forlorn, self-hating, emotionally inert creature, the contemporary cancer personality. As far as I know, no oncologist convinced of the efficacy of polychemo-therapy and immunotherapy in treating patients has contributed to the fictions about a specific cancer per-sonality. Needless to say, the hypothesis that distress can affect immunological responsiveness (and, in some circumstances, lower immunity to disease) is hardly the same as—or constitutes evidence for—the view that

52

emotions cause diseases, much less for the belief that specific emotions can produce specific diseases.

Recent conjecture about the modern cancer character type finds its true antecedent and counterpart in the literature on TB, where the same theory, put in similar terms, had long been in circulation. In his *Morbidus Anglicus* (1672), Gideon Harvey declared "melancholy" and "choler" to be "the sole cause" of TB (for which he used the metaphoric term "corrosion"). In 1881, a year before Robert Koch published his paper announcing the discovery of the tubercle bacillus and demonstrating that it was the primary cause of the disease, a standard medical textbook gave as the causes of tuberculosis: hereditary disposition, unfavorable climate, sedentary indoor life, defective ventilation, deficiency of light, and "depressing emotions."* Though the entry had to be changed for the next edition, it took a long time for these notions to lose credibility. "I'm mentally ill, the disease of the lungs is nothing but an overflowing of my mental disease," Kafka wrote to Milena in 1920. Applied to TB, the theory that emotions cause diseases survived well into this century—until, finally, it was discovered how to cure the disease. The theory's fashionable current application—which relates cancer to emotional withdrawal and lack of self-confidence and confidence in the future—is likely to prove more tenable than its application to tuberculosis.

•

* August Flint and William H. Welch, *The Principles and Practice of Medicine* (fifth edition, 1881), cited in René and Jean Dubos, *The White Plague* (1952).

In the plague-ridden England of the late sixteenth and seventeenth centuries, according to the historian Keith Thomas, it was widely believed that "the happy man would not get plague." The fantasy that a happy state of mind would fend off disease probably flourished for all infectious diseases, before the nature of infection was understood. Theories that diseases are caused by mental states and can be cured by will power are always an index of how much is not understood about the physical terrain of a disease.

Moreover, there is a peculiarly modern predilection for psychological explanations of disease, as of everything else. Psychologizing seems to provide control over the experiences and events (like grave illnesses) over which people have in fact little or no control. Psychological understanding undermines the "reality" of a disease. That reality has to be explained. (It really means; or is a symbol of; or must be interpreted so.) For those who live neither with religious consolations about death nor with a sense of death (or of anything else) as natural, death is the obscene mystery, the ultimate affront, the thing that cannot be controlled. It can only be denied. A large part of the popularity and persuasiveness of psychology comes from its being a sublimated spiritualism: a secular, ostensibly scentific way of affirming the primacy of "spirit" over matter. That ineluctably material reality, disease, can be given a psychological explanation. Death itself can be considered, ultimately, a psychological phenomenon. Groddeck declared in *The Book of the It* (he was speaking of TB): "He alone will die who wishes to die, to whom life is intolerable." The promise of a temporary triumph over

54

death is implicit in much of the psychological thinking that starts from Freud and Jung.

At the least, there is the promise of a triumph over illness. A "physical" illness becomes in a way less real —but, in compensation, more interesting—so far as it can be considered a "mental" one. Speculation throughout the modern period has tended steadily to enlarge the category of mental illness. Indeed, part of the denial of death in this culture is a vast expansion of the category of illness as such.

Illness expands by means of two hypotheses. The first is that every form of social deviation can be considered an illness. Thus, if criminal behavior can be considered an illness, then criminals are not to be condemned or punished but to be understood (as a doctor understands), treated, cured.* The second is that every illness can be considered psychologically. Illness is interpreted as, basically, a psychological event, and people are encouraged to believe that they get sick because they (unconsciously) want to, and that they can cure themselves by the mobilization of will; that they can choose not to die of the disease. These two hypotheses are complementary. As the first seems to relieve guilt, the second reinstates it. Psychological theories of illness are a powerful means of

* An early statement of this view, now so much on the defensive, is in Samuel Butler's *Erewhon* (1872). Butler's way of suggesting that criminality was a disease, like TB, that was either hereditary or the result of an unwholesome environment was to point out the absurdity of condemning the sick. In Erewhon, those who murdered or stole are sympathetically treated as ill persons, while tuberculosis is punished as a crime.

placing the blame on the ill. Patients who are instructed that they have, unwittingly, caused their disease are also being made to feel that they have deserved it.

8

Punitive notions of disease have a long history, and such notions are particularly active with cancer. There is the "fight" or "crusade" against cancer; cancer is the "killer" disease; people who have cancer are "cancer victims." Ostensibly, the illness is the culprit. But it is also the cancer patient who is made culpable. Widely believed psychological theories of disease assign to the luckless ill the ultimate responsibility both for falling ill and for getting well. And conventions of treating cancer as no mere disease but a demonic enemy make cancer not just a lethal disease but a shameful one.

Leprosy in its heyday aroused a similarly disproportionate sense of horror. In the Middle Ages, the leper was a social text in which corruption was made visible; an exemplum, an emblem of decay. Nothing is more punitive than to give a disease a meaning—that meaning being invariably a moralistic one. Any important disease whose causality is murky, and for which treatment is ineffectual, tends to be awash in significance. First, the subjects of deepest dread (corruption, decay, pollution, anomie, weakness) are identified with the disease. The disease itself becomes a metaphor. Then, in the name of the disease (that is, using it as a metaphor), that horror is imposed on other things. The disease becomes adjectival. Something is said to be disease-like, meaning that it is disgusting or ugly. In French, a moldering stone façade is still *lépreuse*.

Epidemic diseases were a common figure for social disorder. From pestilence (bubonic plague) came "pestilent," whose figurative meaning, according to the *Oxford English Dictionary*, is "injurious to religion, morals, or public peace—1513"; and "pestilential," meaning "morally baneful or pernicious—1531." Feelings about evil are projected onto a disease. And the disease (so enriched with meanings) is projected onto the world.

•

In the past, such grandiloquent fantasies were regularly attached to the epidemic diseases, diseases that were a collective calamity. In the last two centuries, the diseases most often used as metaphors for evil were syphilis, tuberculosis, and cancer—all diseases imagined to be, preeminently, the diseases of individuals.

Syphilis was thought to be not only a horrible disease but a demeaning, vulgar one. Anti-democrats used it to evoke the desecrations of an egalitarian age. Baudelaire, in a note for his never completed book on Belgium, wrote:

We all have the republican spirit in our veins, like syphilis in our bones—we are democraticized and venerealized.

58

In the sense of an infection that corrupts morally and debilitates physically, syphilis was to become a standard trope in late-nineteenth- and early-twentieth-century anti-Semitic polemics. In 1933 Wilhelm Reich argued that "the irrational fear of syphilis was one of the major sources of National Socialism's political views and its anti-Semitism." But although he perceived sexual and political phobias being projected onto a disease in the grisly harping on syphilis in *Mein Kampf*, it never occurred to Reich how much was being projected in his own persistent use of cancer as a metaphor for the ills of the modern era. Indeed, cancer can be stretched much further than syphilis can as a metaphor.

Syphilis was limited as a metaphor because the disease itself was not regarded as mysterious; only awful. A tainted heredity (Ibsen's *Ghosts*), the perils of sex (Charles-Louis Philippe's *Bubu de Montparnasse*, Mann's *Doctor Faustus*)—there was horror aplenty in syphilis. But no mystery. Its causality was clear, and understood to be singular. Syphilis was the grimmest of gifts, "transmitted" or "carried" by a sometimes ignorant sender to the unsuspecting receiver. In contrast, TB was regarded as a mysterious affliction, and a disease with myriad causes—just as today, while everyone acknowledges cancer to be an unsolved riddle, it is also generally agreed that cancer is multi-determined. A variety of factors—such as cancer-causing substances ("carcinogens") in the environment, genetic makeup, lowering of immunodefenses (by previous illness or emotional trauma), characterological predisposition— are held responsible for the disease. And many researchers assert that cancer is not one but more than a hundred clinically distinct diseases, that each cancer

59

has to be studied separately, and that what will eventually be developed is an array of cures, one for each of the different cancers.

The resemblance of current ideas about cancer's myriad causes to long-held but now discredited views about TB suggests the possibility that cancer may be one disease after all and that it may turn out, as TB did, to have a principal causal agent and be controllable by one program of treatment. Indeed, as Lewis Thomas has observed, all the diseases for which the issue of causation has been settled, and which can be prevented and cured, have turned out to have a simple physical cause—like the pneumococcus for pneumonia, the tubercle bacillus for tuberculosis, a single vitamin deficiency for pellagra—and it is far from unlikely that something comparable will eventually be isolated for cancer. The notion that a disease can be explained only by a variety of causes is precisely characteristic of thinking about diseases whose causation is *not* understood. And it is diseases thought to be multi-determined (that is, mysterious) that have the widest possibilities as metaphors for what is felt to be socially or morally wrong.

•

TB and cancer have been used to express not only (like syphilis) crude fantasies about contamination but also fairly complex feelings about strength and weakness, and about energy. For more than a century and a half, tuberculosis provided a metaphoric equivalent for delicacy, sensitivity, sadness, powerlessness; while whatever seemed ruthless, implacable, predatory, could be analogized to cancer. (Thus, Baudelaire in 1852, in his essay *"L'Ecole païenne,"* observed: "A frenzied passion for art is a canker that devours the rest. . . .") TB was an ambivalent metaphor, both a scourge and an emblem of refinement. Cancer was never viewed other than as a scourge; it was, metaphorically, the barbarian within.

While syphilis was thought to be passively incurred, an entirely involuntary disaster, TB was once, and cancer is now, thought to be a pathology of energy, a disease of the will. Concern about energy and feeling, fears about the havoc they wreak, have been attached to both diseases. Getting TB was thought to signify a defective vitality, or vitality misspent. "There was a great want of vital power . . . and great constitutional weakness"—so Dickens described little Paul in *Dombey and Son*. The Victorian idea of TB as a disease of low energy (and heightened sensitivity) has its exact complement in the Reichian idea of cancer as a disease of unexpected energy (and anesthetized feelings). In an era in which there seemed to be no inhibitions on being productive, people were anxious about not having enough energy. In our own era of destructive overproduction by the economy and of increasing bureaucratic restraints on the individual, there is both a fear of having too much energy and an anxiety about energy not being allowed to be expressed.

Like Freud's scarcity-economics theory of "instincts," the fantasies about TB which arose in the last century (and lasted well into ours) echo the attitudes of early capitalist accumulation. One has a limited amount of energy, which must be properly spent. (Having an orgasm, in nineteenth-century English slang, was not "coming" but "spending.") Energy, like savings, can be depleted, can run out or be used up, through reckless expenditure. The body will start "consuming" itself, the patient will "waste away."

The language used to describe cancer evokes a different economic catastrophe: that of unregulated, abnormal, incoherent growth. The tumor has energy, not the patient; "it" is out of control. Cancer cells, according to the textbook account, are cells that have shed the mechanism which "restrains" growth. (The growth of normal cells is "self-limiting," due to a mechanism called "contact inhibition.") Cells without inhibitions, cancer cells will continue to grow and extend over each other in a "chaotic" fashion, destroying the body's normal cells, architecture, and functions.

Early capitalism assumes the necessity of regulated spending, saving, accounting, discipline—an economy that depends on the rational limitation of desire. TB is described in images that sum up the negative behavior of nineteenth-century *homo economicus*: consumption; wasting; squandering of vitality. Advanced capitalism requires expansion, speculation, the creation of new needs (the problem of satisfaction and dissatisfaction); buying on credit; mobility—an economy that depends on the irrational indulgence of desire. Cancer is described in images that sum up the negative behavior of twentieth-century *homo economicus*: abnormal growth; repression of energy, that is, refusal to consume or spend.

•

TB was understood, like insanity, to be a kind of one-sidedness: a failure of will or an overintensity. However much the disease was dreaded, TB always had pathos. Like the mental patient today, the tubercular was considered to be someone quintessentially vulnerable, and full of self-destructive whims. Nineteenth- and early-twentieth-century physicians addressed themselves to coaxing their tubercular patients back to health. Their prescription was the same as the enlightened one for mental patients today: cheerful surroundings, isolation from stress and family, healthy diet, exercise, rest.

The understanding of cancer supports quite different, avowedly brutal notions of treatment. (A common cancer hospital witticism, heard as often from doctors as from patients: "The treatment is worse than the disease.") There can be no question of pampering the patient. With the patient's body considered to be under attack ("invasion"), the only treatment is counterattack.

The controlling metaphors in descriptions of cancer are, in fact, drawn not from economics but from the language of warfare: every physician and every attentive patient is familiar with, if perhaps inured to, this military terminology. Thus, cancer cells do not simply multiply; they are "invasive." ("Malignant tumors invade even when they grow very slowly," as one textbook puts it.) Cancer cells "colonize" from the original tumor to far sites in the body, first setting up tiny outposts ("micrometastases") whose presence is assumed, though they cannot be detected. Rarely are the body's "defenses" vigorous enough to obliterate a tumor that has established its own blood supply and consists of billions of destructive cells. However "radical" the surgical intervention, however many "scans" are taken of the body landscape, most remissions are temporary; the prospects are that "tumor invasion" will continue, or that rogue cells will eventually regroup and mount a new assault on the organism.

Treatment also has a military flavor. Radiotherapy uses the metaphors of aerial warfare; patients are "bombarded" with toxic rays. And chemotherapy is chemical warfare, using poisons.* Treatment aims to "kill" cancer cells (without, it is hoped, killing the patient). Unpleasant side effects to treatment are advertised, indeed overadvertised. ("The agony of chemotherapy" is a standard phrase.) It is impossible to avoid damaging or destroying healthy cells (indeed, some methods used to treat cancer can cause cancer), but it is thought that nearly any damage to the body is justified if it saves the patient's life. Often, of course, it doesn't work. (As in: "We had to destroy Ben Suc in order to save it.") There is everything but the body count.

The military metaphor in medicine first came into wide use in the 1880s, with the identification of bac-

* Drugs of the nitrogen mustard type (so-called alkylating agents)—like cyclophosphamide (Cytoxan)—were the first generation of cancer drugs. Their use with leukemia (which is characterized by an excessive production of immature white cells), then with other forms of cancer—was suggested by an inadvertent experiment with chemical warfare toward the end of World War II, when an American ship, loaded with nitrogen mustard gas, was blown up in the Naples harbor, and many of the sailors died of their lethally low white-cell and platelet counts (that is, of bone-marrow poisoning) rather than of burns or sea-water inhalation.

Chemotherapy and weaponry seem to go together, if only as a fancy. The first modern chemotherapy success was with syphilis: in 1910, Paul Ehrlich introduced an arsenic derivative, arsphenamine (Salvarsan), which was called "the magic bullet."

teria as agents of disease. Bacteria were said to "invade" or "infiltrate." But talk of siege and war to describe disease now has, with cancer, a striking literalness and authority. Not only is the clinical course of the disease and its medical treatment thus described, but the disease itself is conceived as the enemy on which society wages war. More recently, the fight against cancer has sounded like a colonial war—with similarly vast appropriations of government money—and in a decade when colonial wars haven't gone too well, this militarized rhetoric seems to be backfiring. Pessimism among doctors about the efficacy of treatment is growing, in spite of the strong advances in chemotherapy and immunotherapy made since 1970. Reporters covering "the war on cancer" frequently caution the public to distinguish between official fictions and harsh facts; a few years ago, one science writer found American Cancer Society proclamations that cancer is curable and progress has been made "reminiscent of Vietnam optimism prior to the deluge." Still, it is one thing to be skeptical about the rhetoric that surrounds cancer, another to give support to many uninformed doctors who insist that no significant progress in treatment has been made, and that cancer is not really curable. The bromides of the American cancer establishment, tirelessly hailing the imminent victory over cancer; the professional pessimism of a large number of cancer specialists, talking like battle-weary officers mired down in an interminable colonial war—these are twin distortions in this military rhetoric about cancer.

•

Other distortions follow with the extension of cancer images in more grandiose schemes of warfare. As TB was represented as the spiritualizing of consciousness, cancer is understood as the overwhelming or obliterating of consciousness (by a mindless It). In TB, you are eating yourself up, being refined, getting down to the core, the real you. In cancer, non-intelligent ("primitive," "embryonic," "atavistic") cells are multiplying, and you are being replaced by the nonyou. Immunologists class the body's cancer cells as "nonself."

It is worth noting that Reich, who did more than anyone else to disseminate the psychological theory of cancer, also found something equivalent to cancer in the biosphere.

> There is a deadly orgone energy. It is in the atmosphere. You can demonstrate it on devices such as the Geiger counter. It's a swampy quality. . . . Stagnant, deadly water which doesn't flow, doesn't metabolize. Cancer, too, is due to the stagnation of the flow of the life energy of the organism.

Reich's language has its own inimitable coherence. And more and more—as its metaphoric uses gain in credibility—cancer is felt to be what he thought it was, a cosmic disease, the emblem of all the destructive, alien powers to which the organism is host.

As TB was the disease of the sick self, cancer is the disease of the Other. Cancer proceeds by a science-fiction scenario: an invasion of "alien" or "mutant" cells, stronger than normal cells (*Invasion of the Body Snatchers, The Incredible Shrinking Man, The Blob, The Thing*). One standard science-fiction plot is mutation, either mutants arriving from outer space or ac-

66

cidental mutations among humans. Cancer could be described as a triumphant mutation, and mutation is now mainly an image for cancer. As a theory of the psychological genesis of cancer, the Reichian imagery of energy checked, not allowed to move outward, then turned back on itself, driving cells beserk, is already the stuff of science fiction. And Reich's image of death in the air—of deadly energy that registers on a Geiger counter—suggests how much the science-fiction images about cancer (a disease that comes from deadly rays, and is treated by deadly rays) echo the collective nightmare. The original fear about exposure to atomic radiation was genetic deformities in the next generation; that was replaced by another fear, as statistics started to show much higher cancer rates among Hiroshima and Nagasaki survivors and their descendants.

Cancer is a metaphor for what is most ferociously energetic; and these energies constitute the ultimate insult to natural order. In a science-fiction tale by Tommaso Landolfi, the spaceship is called "Cancerqueen." (It is hardly within the range of the tuberculosis metaphor that a writer could have imagined an intrepid vessel named "Consumptionqueen.") When not being explained away as something psychological, buried in the recesses of the self, cancer is being magnified and projected into a metaphor for the biggest enemy, the furthest goal. Thus, Nixon's bid to match Kennedy's promise to put Americans on the moon was, appropriately enough, the promise to "conquer" cancer. Both were science-fiction ventures. The equivalent of the legislation establishing the space program was the National Cancer Act of 1971, which did not envisage the near-to-hand decisions that could bring under control the industrial economy that pollutes—only the great destination: the cure.

TB was a disease in the service of a romantic view of the world. Cancer is now in the service of a simplistic view of the world that can turn paranoid. The disease is often experienced as a form of demonic possession—tumors are "malignant" or "benign," like forces—and many terrified cancer patients are disposed to seek out faith healers, to be exorcised. The main organized support for dangerous nostrums like Laetrile comes from far-right groups to whose politics of paranoia the fantasy of a miracle cure for cancer makes a serviceable addition, along with a belief in UFOs. (The John Birch Society distributes a forty-five-minute film called *World Without Cancer*.) For the more sophisticated, cancer signifies the rebellion of the injured ecosphere: Nature taking revenge on a wicked technocratic world. False hopes and simplified terrors are raised by crude statistics brandished for the general public, such as that 90 percent of all cancers are "environmentally caused," or that imprudent diet and tobacco smoking alone account for 75 percent of all cancer deaths. To the accompaniment of this numbers game (it is difficult to see how any statistics about "all cancers" or "all cancer deaths" could be defended), cigarettes, hair dyes, bacon, saccharine, hormone-fed poultry, pesticides, low-sulphur coal—a lengthening roll call of products we take for granted have been found to cause cancer. X-rays give cancer (the treatment meant to cure kills); so do emanations from the television set and the microwave oven and the fluorescent clock face. As with syphilis, an innocent or trivial act—or exposure— in the present can have dire consequences far in the future. It is also known that cancer rates are high for workers in a large number of industrial occupations. Though the exact processes of causation lying behind the statistics remain unknown, it seems clear that many cancers are preventable. But cancer is not just a disease ushered in by the Industrial Revolution (there was cancer in Arcadia) and certainly more than the sin of capitalism (within their more limited industrial capacities, the Russians pollute worse than we do). The widespread current view of cancer as a disease of industrial civilization is as unsound scientifically as the right-wing fantasy of a "world without cancer" (like a world without subversives). Both rest on the mistaken feeling that cancer is a distinctively "modern" disease.

The medieval experience of the plague was firmly tied to notions of moral pollution, and people invariably looked for a scapegoat external to the stricken community. (Massacres of Jews in unprecedented numbers took place everywhere in plague-stricken Europe of 1347–48, then stopped as soon as the plague receded.) With the modern diseases, the scapegoat is not so easily separated from the patient. But much as these diseases individualize, they also pick up some of the metaphors of epidemic diseases. (Diseases understood to be simply epidemic have become less useful as metaphors, as evidenced by the near-total historical amnesia about the influenza pandemic of 1918–19, in which more people died than in the four years of World War I.) Presently, it is as much a cliché to say that cancer is "environmentally" caused as it was—and still is—to say that it is caused by mismanaged emotions. TB was associated with pollution (Florence Nightingale thought it was "induced by the foul air of houses"), and now cancer is thought of as a disease of the contamination of the whole world. TB was "the white plague." With awareness of environmental pollution, people have started saying that there is an "epidemic" or "plague" of cancer.

9

Illnesses have always been used as metaphors to enliven charges that a society was corrupt or unjust. Traditional disease metaphors are principally a way of being vehement; they are, compared with the modern metaphors, relatively contentless. Shakespeare does many variations on a standard form of the metaphor, an infection in the "body politic"—making no distinction between a contagion, an infection, a sore, an abscess, an ulcer, and what we would call a tumor. For purposes of invective, diseases are of only two types: the painful but curable, and the possibly fatal. Particular diseases figure as examples of diseases in general; no disease has its own distinctive logic. Disease imagery is used to express concern for social order, and health is something everyone is presumed to know about. Such metaphors do not project the modern idea of a specific master illness, in which what is at issue is health itself.

Master illnesses like TB and cancer are more specifically polemical. They are used to propose new, critical standards of individual health, and to express a sense of dissatisfaction with society as such. Unlike the Elizabethan metaphors—which complain of some general aberration of public calamity that is, in consequence, dislocating to individuals—the modern metaphors suggest a profound disequilibrium between individual and society, with a society conceived as the individual's adversary. Disease metaphors are used to judge society not as out of balance but as repressive. They turn up regularly in Romantic rhetoric which opposes heart to head, spontaneity to reason, nature to artifice, country to city.

When travel to a better climate was invented as a treatment for TB in the early nineteenth century, the most contradictory destinations were proposed. The south, mountains, deserts, islands—their very diversity suggests what they have in common: the rejection of the city. In *La Traviata,* as soon as Alfredo wins Violetta's love, he moves her from unhealthy wicked Paris to the wholesome countryside: instant health follows. And Violetta's giving up on happiness is tantamount to leaving the country and returning to the city—where her doom is sealed, her TB returns, and she dies.

The metaphor of cancer expands the theme of the rejection of the city. Before it was understood as, literally, a cancer-causing (carcinogenic) environment, the city was seen as itself a cancer—a place of abnormal, unnatural growth. In *The Living City* (1958), Frank Lloyd Wright compared the city of earlier times, a healthy organism. ("The city then was not malignant"), with the modern city. "To look at the cross-section of

72

any plan of a big city is to look at the section of a fibrous tumor."*

Throughout the nineteenth century, disease metaphors become more virulent, preposterous, demagogic. And there is an increasing tendency to call any situation one disapproves of a disease. Disease, which could be considered as much a part of nature as is health, became the synonym of whatever was "unnatural." In *Les Misérables,* Hugo wrote:

> Monasticism, such as it existed in Spain and as it exists in Tibet, is for civilization a sort of tuberculosis. It cuts off life. Quite simply, it depopulates. Confinement, castration. It was a scourge in Europe.

Bichat in 1800 defined life as "the ensemble of functions which resists death." That contrast between life and death was to be transferred to a contrast between life and disease. Disease (now equated with death) is what opposes life.

In 1916, in "Socialism and Culture," Gramsci denounced

> the habit of thinking that culture is encyclopedic knowledge. . . . This form of culture serves to create

* The sociologist Herbert Gans has called my attention to the importance of tuberculosis and the alleged or real threat of it in the slum-clearing and "model tenament" movements of the late nineteenth and early twentieth centuries, the feeling being that slum housing "bred" TB. The shift from TB to cancer in planning and housing rhetoric had taken place by the 1950s. "Blight" (a virtual synonym for slum) is seen as a cancer that spreads insidiously, and the use of the term "invasion" to describe when the non-white and poor move into a middle-class neighborhood is as much a metaphor borrowed from cancer as from the military: the two discourses overlap.

73

that pale and broken-winded intellectualism . . . which has produced a whole crowd of boasters and day-dreamers more harmful to a healthy social life than tuberculosis or syphilis microbes are to the body's beauty and health. . . .

In 1919, Mandelstam paid the following tribute to Pasternak:

> To read Pasternak's verse is to clear one's throat, to fortify one's breathing, to fill one's lungs; such poetry must be healthy, a cure for tuberculosis. No poetry is healthier at the present moment. It is like drinking *koumiss* after canned American milk.

And Marinetti, denouncing Communism in 1920:

> Communism is the exasperation of the bureaucratic cancer that has always wasted humanity. A German cancer, a product of the characteristic German prepa-rationism. Every pedantic preparation is anti-hu-man. . . .

It is for the same iniquity that the protofascist Italian writer attacks Communism and the future founder of the Italian Communist Party attacks a certain bour-geois idea of culture ("truly harmful, especially to the proletariat," Gramsci says)—for being artificial, pe-dantic, rigid, lifeless. Both TB and cancer have been regularly invoked to condemn repressive practices and ideals, repression being conceived of as an environment that deprives one of strength (TB) or of flexibility and spontaneity (cancer). Modern disease metaphors specify an ideal of society's well-being, analogized to physical health, that is as frequently anti-political as it is a call for a new political order.

●

Order is the oldest concern of political philosophy, and if it is plausible to compare the polis to an organism, then it is plausible to compare civil disorder to an illness. The classical formulations which analogize a political disorder to an illness—from Plato to, say, Hobbes—presuppose the classical medical (and political) idea of balance. Illness comes from imbalance. Treatment is aimed at restoring the right balance—in political terms, the right hierarchy. The prognosis is always, in principle, optimistic. Society, by definition, never catches a fatal disease.

When a disease image is used by Machiavelli, the presumption is that the disease can be cured. "Consumption," he wrote,

> in the commencement is easy to cure, and difficult to understand; but when it has neither been discovered in due time, nor treated upon a proper principle, it becomes easy to understand, and difficult to cure. The same thing happens in state affairs, by foreseeing them at a distance, which is only done by men of talents, the evils which might arise from them are soon cured; but when, from want of foresight, they are suffered to increase to such a height that they are perceptible to everyone, there is no longer any remedy.

Machiavelli invokes TB as a disease whose progress can be cut off, if it is detected at an early stage (when its symptoms are barely visible). Given proper foresight, the course of a disease is not irreversible; the same for disturbances in the body politic. Machiavelli offers an illness metaphor that is not so much about society as about statecraft (conceived as a therapeutic art): as prudence is needed to control serious diseases, so foresight is needed to control social crises. It is a metaphor about foresight, and a call to foresight.

In political philosophy's great tradition, the analogy between disease and civil disorder is proposed to encourage rulers to pursue a more rational policy. "Although nothing can be immortall, which mortals make," Hobbes wrote,

> yet, if men had the use of reason they pretend to, their Commonwealths might be secured, at least, from perishing by internal diseases. . . . Therefore when they come to be dissolved, not by externall violence, but intestine disorder, the fault is not in men, as they are the *Matter*; but as they are the *Makers*, and orderers of them.

Hobbes's view is anything but fatalistic. Rulers have the responsibility and the ability (through reason) to control disorder. For Hobbes, murder ("externall violence") is the only "natural" way for a society or institution to die. To perish from internal disorder—analogized to a disease—is suicide, something quite preventable; an act of will, or rather a failure of will (that is, of reason).

The disease metaphor was used in political philosophy to reinforce the call for a rational response. Machiavelli and Hobbes fixed on one part of medical wisdom, the importance of cutting off serious disease early, while it is relatively easy to control. The disease metaphor could also be used to encourage rulers to another kind of foresight. In 1708, Lord Shaftesbury wrote:

> There are certain humours in mankind which of necessity must have vent. The human mind and body are both of them naturally subject to commotions . . . as there are strange ferments in the blood, which in many bodies occasion an extra-ordinary discharge. . . . Should physicians endeavour absolutely to allay those ferments of the body, and strike in the humours which discover themselves in such eruptions, they might, instead of making a cure, bid fair perhaps to raise a plague, and turn a spring-ague or an autumn-surfeit into an epidemical malignant fever. They are certainly as ill physicians in the body politic who would needs be tampering with these mental eruptions, and, under the specious pretence of healing this itch of superstition and saving souls from the contagion of enthusiasm, should set all nature in an uproar, and turn a few innocent carbuncles into an inflammation and mortal gangrene.

Shaftesbury's point is that it is rational to tolerate a certain amount of irrationality ("superstition," "enthusiasm"), and that stern repressive measures are likely to aggravate disorder rather than cure it, turning a nuisance into a disaster. The body politic should not be overmedicalized; a remedy should not be sought for every disorder.

For Machiavelli, foresight; for Hobbes, reason; for Shaftesbury, tolerance—these are all ideas of how proper statecraft, conceived on a medical analogy, can prevent a fatal disorder. Society is presumed to be in basically good health; disease (disorder) is, in principle, always manageable.

●

In the modern period, the use of disease imagery in political rhetoric implies other, less lenient assumptions. The modern idea of revolution, based on an estimate of the unremitting bleakness of the existing political situation, shattered the old, optimistic use of disease metaphors. John Adams wrote in his diary, in December 1772:

> The Prospect before me . . . is very gloomy. My Country is in deep Distress, and has very little Ground of Hope. . . . The Body of the People seem to be worn out, by struggling, and Venality, Servility and Prostitution, eat and spread like a Cancer.

Political events started commonly to be defined as being unprecedented, radical; and eventually both civil disturbances and wars come to be understood as, really, revolutions. As might be expected, it was not with the American but with the French Revolution that disease metaphors in the modern sense came into their own—particularly in the conservative response to the French Revolution. In *Reflections on the Revolution in France* (1790), Edmund Burke contrasted older wars and civil disturbances with this one, which he considered to have a totally new character. Before, no matter what the disaster, "the organs . . . of the state, however shattered, existed." But, he addressed the French, "your present confusion, like a palsy, has attacked the fountain of life itself."

As classical theories of the polis have gone the way of the theories of the four humours, so a modern idea of politics has been complemented by a modern idea of disease. Disease equals death. Burke invoked palsy (and "the living ulcer of a corroding memory"). The emphasis was soon to be on diseases that are loathsome and fatal. Such diseases are not to be managed or treated; they are to be attacked. In Hugo's novel about the French Revolution, *Quatre-vingt-treize* (1874), the revolutionary Gauvain, condemned to the guillotine, absolves the Revolution with all its bloodshed, including his own imminent execution,

> because it is a storm. A storm always knows what it is doing. . . . Civilization was in the grip of plague; this gale comes to the rescue. Perhaps it is not selective enough. Can it act otherwise? It is entrusted with the arduous task of sweeping away disease! In face of the horrible infection, I understand the fury of the blast.

It is hardly the last time that revolutionary violence would be justified on the grounds that society has a radical, horrible illness. The melodramatics of the disease metaphor in modern political discourse assume a punitive notion: of the disease not as a punishment but as a sign of evil, something to be punished.

Modern totalitarian movements, whether of the right or of the left, have been peculiarly—and revealingly—inclined to use disease imagery. The Nazis declared that someone of mixed "racial" origin was like a syphilitic. European Jewry was repeatedly analogized to syphilis, and to a cancer that must be excised. Disease metaphors were a staple of Bolshevik polemics, and Trotsky, the most gifted of all communist polemicists, used them with the greatest profusion—particularly after his banishment from the Soviet Union in 1929. Stalinism was called a cholera, a syphilis, and a cancer.* To use only fatal diseases for imagery in politics gives the metaphor a much more pointed character. Now, to liken a political event or situation to an illness is to impute guilt, to prescribe punishment.

This is particularly true of the use of cancer as a metaphor. It amounts to saying, first of all, that the event or situation is unqualifiedly and unredeemably wicked. It enormously ups the ante. Hitler, in his first political tract, an anti-Semitic diatribe written in September 1919, accused the Jews of producing "a racial tuberculosis among nations."† Tuberculosis still re-

* Cf. Isaac Deutscher, *The Prophet Outcast: Trotsky, 1929–1940* (1963): " 'Certain measures,' Trotsky wrote to [Philip] Rahv [on March 21, 1938], 'are necessary for a struggle against incorrect theory, and others for fighting a cholera epidemic. Stalin is incomparably nearer to cholera than to a false theory. The struggle must be intense, truculent, merciless. An element of "fanaticism" . . . is salutary.' " And: "Trotsky spoke of the 'syphilis of Stalinism' or of the 'cancer that must be burned out of the labour movement with a hot iron.'. . ."

Notably, Solzhenitsyn's *Cancer Ward* contains virtually no uses of cancer as a metaphor—for Stalinism, or for anything else. Solzhenitsyn was not misrepresenting his novel when, hoping to get it published in the Soviet Union, he told the Board of the Union of Writers in 1967 that the title was not "some kind of symbol," as was being charged, and that "the subject is specifically and literally cancer."

† "[The Jew's] power is the power of money which in the form of interest effortlessly and interminably multiples itself in his hands and forces upon nations that most dangerous of yokes. . . . Everything which makes men strive for higher things, whether religion, socialism, or democracy, is for him only a means to an end, to the satisfaction of a lust for money and domination. His activities produce a racial tuberculosis among nations. . . ." A late-nineteenth-century precursor of

tained its prestige as the overdetermined, culpable illness of the nineteeth century. (Recall Hugo's comparison of monasticism with TB.) But the Nazis quickly modernized their rhetoric, and indeed the imagery of cancer was far more apt for their purposes. As was said in speeches about "the Jewish problem" throughout the 1930s, to treat a cancer, one must cut out much of the healthy tissue around it. The imagery of cancer for the Nazis prescribes "radical" treatment, in contrast to the "soft" treatment thought appropriate for TB—the difference between sanatoria (that is, exile) and surgery (that is, crematoria). (The Jews were also identified with, and became a metaphor for, city life—with Nazi rhetoric echoing all the Romantic clichés about cities as a debilitating, merely cerebral, morally contaminated, unhealthy environment.)

To describe a phenomenon as a cancer is an incitement to violence. The use of cancer in political discourse encourages fatalism and justifies "severe" measures—as well as strongly reinforcing the widespread notion that the disease is necessarily fatal. The concept of disease is never innocent. But it could be argued that the cancer metaphors are in themselves implicitly genocidal. No specific political view seems to have a monopoly on this metaphor. Trotsky called Stalinism the cancer of Marxism; in China in the last year, the Gang of Four have become, among other things, "the cancer of China." John Dean explained Watergate to Nixon:

Nazi ideology, Julius Langbehn, called the Jews "only a passing pest and cholera." But in Hitler's TB image there is already something easily transferred to cancer: the idea that Jewish power "effortlessly and interminably multiplies."

"We have a cancer within—close to the Presidency—that's growing." The standard metaphor of Arab polemics—heard by Israelis on the radio every day for the last twenty years—is that Israel is "a cancer in the heart of the Arab world" or "the cancer of the Middle East," and an officer with the Christian Lebanese rightist forces besieging the Palestine refugee camp of Tal Zaatar in August 1976 called the camp "a cancer in the Lebanese body." The cancer metaphor seems hard to resist for those who wish to register indignation. Thus, Neal Ascherson wrote in 1969 that the Slansky Affair "was—is—a huge cancer in the body of the Czechoslovak state and nation"; Simon Leys, in *Chinese Shadows,* speaks of "the Maoist cancer that is gnawing away at the face of China"; D. H. Lawrence called masturbation "the deepest and most dangerous cancer of our civilization"; and I once wrote, in the heat of despair over America's war on Vietnam, that "the white race is the cancer of human history."

But how to be morally severe in the late twentieth century? How, when there is so much to be severe about; how, when we have a sense of evil but no longer the religious or philosophical language to talk intelligently about evil. Trying to comprehend "radical" or "absolute" evil, we search for adequate metaphors. But the modern disease metaphors are all cheap shots. The people who have the real disease are also hardly helped by hearing their disease's name constantly being dropped as the epitome of evil. Only in the most limited sense is any historical event or problem like an illness. And the cancer metaphor is particularly crass. It is invariably an encouragement to

82

simplify what is complex and an invitation to self-righteousness, if not to fanaticism.

It is instructive to compare the image of cancer with that of gangrene. With some of the same metaphoric properties as cancer—it starts from nothing; it spreads; it is disgusting—gangrene would seem to be laden with everything a polemicist would want. Indeed, it was used in one important moral polemic—against the French use of torture in Algeria in the 1950s; the title of the famous book exposing that torture was called *La Gangrène*. But there is a large difference between the cancer and the gangrene metaphors. First, causality is clear with gangrene. It is external (gangrene can develop from a scratch); cancer is understood as mysterious, a disease with multiple causes, internal as well as external. Second, gangrene is not as all-encompassing a disaster. It leads often to amputation, less often to death; cancer is presumed to lead to death in most cases. Not gangrene—and not the plague (despite the notable attempts by writers as different as Artaud, Reich, and Camus to impose that as a metaphor for the dismal and the disastrous)—but cancer remains the most radical of disease metaphors. And just because it is so radical, it is particularly tendentious—a good metaphor for paranoids, for those who need to turn campaigns into crusades, for the fatalistic (cancer = death), and for those under the spell of ahistorical revolutionary optimism (the idea that only the most radical changes are desirable). As long as so much militaristic hyperbole attaches to the description and treatment of cancer, it is a particularly unapt metaphor for the peace-loving.

It is, of course, likely that the language about cancer will evolve in the coming years. It must change, decisively, when the disease is finally understood and the rate of cure becomes much higher. It is already changing, with the development of new forms of treatment. As chemotherapy is more and more supplanting radiation in the treatment of cancer patients, an effective form of treatment (already a supplementary treatment of proven use) seems likely to be found in some kind of immunotherapy. Concepts have started to shift in certain medical circles, where doctors are concentrating on the steep buildup of the body's immunological responses to cancer. As the language of treatment evolves from military metaphors of aggressive warfare to metaphors featuring the body's "natural defenses" (what is called the "immunodefensive system" can also—to break entirely with the military metaphor—be called the body's "immune competence"), cancer will be partly de-mythicized; and it may then be possible to compare something to a cancer without implying either a fatalistic diagnosis or a rousing call to fight by any means whatever a lethal, insidious enemy. Then perhaps it will be morally permissible, as it is not now, to use cancer as a metaphor.

But at that time, perhaps nobody will want any longer to compare anything awful to cancer. Since the interest of the metaphor is precisely that it refers to a disease so overlaid with mystification, so charged with the fantasy of inescapable fatality. Since our views about cancer, and the metaphors we have imposed on it, are so much a vehicle for the large insufficiencies of this culture, for our shallow attitude toward death, for our anxieties about feeling, for our reckless improvident responses to our real "problems of growth," for our inability to construct an advanced industrial society which properly regulates consumption, and for our justified fears of the increasingly violent course of history. The cancer metaphor will be made obsolete, I would predict, long before the problems it has reflected so persuasively will be resolved.

ABOUT THE AUTHOR

SUSAN SONTAG is the author of two novels, *The Bene-factor* and *Death Kit*. Her other books include two col-lections of essays, *Against Interpretation* and *Styles of Radical Will*; *On Photography* (winner of the National Book Critics Circle Award for Criticism); and, most recently, *I, etcetera*. She has written and directed three films: *Duet for Cannibals* (1969) and *Brother Carl* (1971), in Sweden, and *Promised Lands* (1974), in Israel.